Gregory Carlyle

A Poetry Collection

*Sparrow in*
*the Machine*

*To my beloved wife,*
*Tara Ann Warner*
*& our children,*
*Kori, Trinity, Journee, and Felicity*

# Table of Contents

# Acknowledgements

I am especially thankful for the contributions
so many have made to my life.

My parents, who despite not having the most
idealistic youths, overcame those obstacles and
placed my brothers and I in a stable home.

To my brothers, Gary and Dwayne,
and my friends from "back in the day", who are still
instrumental in the person I am ever becoming.

My love, my life – know that this piece would not have been
possible without the inspiration and support of my wife,
Tara Ann Warner.

And of course, as always, I am thankful to
My Lord and Savior,
who has found me worthy to be blessed.

# Preface

*Sparrow in the Machine* is an introspective book of poetry
that centers on the primary themes of relationships,
self-actualization, racial inequity, social justice, and love.

The Sparrow represents a vast segment of resilient people that
are living in a world that is beyond their control.

The Machine represents the present-day political
socio-economic environment that is controlled by the few.

I am humbled and pleased to offer to you,
*Sparrow in the Machine.*

# About the Author

 **Gregory Carlyle Warner** is a poet, author and spoken word artist hailing from Hampton Roads, Virginia; currently living and working in the Kansas City Metropolitan area. He is an U.S. Army veteran and holds various degrees from American University, Webster University, and Old Dominion University. His art started to manifest as a young man, but it was through the journey of life, where his unique soulful form of poetic expressions fully matured.

Gregory Carlyle's struggles with love, military life, separation, divorce, and continued battles to be an integral part of his three daughters' lives, proved instrumental in his development and his eventual inner peace.

"My hope is that everyone finds their true purpose in life through living life…the joys, the sorrows, the good, and the bad."

Gregory Carlyle's first published work *100 Years to be Lost: A Poetry Collection* reached #1 in "New Releases for African-American Poetry" on Amazon, where this work remained in the top ten for several weeks. Combined with Gregory Carlyle's personal and professional experiences, this journey takes a new turn exploring recent (and not so recent) societal challenges — political unrest, social upheaval and life changed forever are resounding themes in this latest piece.

In *Sparrow in the Machine,* Gregory Carlyle also has incorporated select poems from his first publication. Following the release of *100 Years to be Lost,* Gregory Carlyle continued to further cultivate these poems and is proud to showcase these legacy works here in his latest collection of poetry.

You can connect with Gregory Carlyle on Instagram (@whole_words) or on Facebook (@WriteItAllDown) where he shares his works in progress and snippets of life adventures with his loving wife Tara.

# Prologue

### *The Sparrow*

"Are not two sparrows sold for a penny?
Yet not one of them will fall
to the ground outside
your Father's care."
**- Matthew 10:29**

### *The Machine*

"But the subjects of the kingdom will be thrown
outside, into the darkness,
where there will be weeping
and gnashing of teeth."
**- Matthew 8:12**

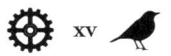

# Sparrow in the Machine

## the Machine

### A Poetry Collection

Gregory Carlyle

# Moonlit Fruit

Under this deep crimson moon
I might die
If I stayed too long
Not too far
In the distance
The tree branches hang low
Heavy from the burden of the freshly hung fruit
The planters are confederated
And always nearby
The stench of their bloodlust
Remains trapped
In this distressed air

Still your breath
And calm your anxiety
As clouds move away
And the moonlight preternaturally creeps
over swooning vegetation
The repeated horror that strangely dominates
This southern landscape is continually revealed

## Darius and Nina

Did y'all ever exhaust the possibilities?
  Or is romance dead?
We watched you like stars across the night sky
Somehow wanting to see ourselves in your love
It was a beautiful, exceptional love
Is she still Oshun?
  or has she now become
    something more ordinary?
I've looked for the *Sanctuary*
  and the beautiful souls in that place
I waited
  but the sequel starring the Lovehalls never came

However, I still like to think that
  Darius and Nina made a place in this world
    with at least one child
      maybe more
        in Chicago or Atlanta—shit even New York
But it's been a while
  and life can fade us all
Who could judge you
  if you fell into the *routine*
    because *that* is real
But if poetry is the possibility of language
  and love impregnates life
We might still see you in the rain
  reclaiming one another
    unapologetically
      once again

# From the Sun, Sincerely Me

**H**ey Mom and Dad,
   I'm writing you from the Sun
   I met a girl here
   and she's sweeter than watermelons in July
   we're getting married tomorrow
   I wish y'all could've made the trip
   I know, I know
   it's all so sudden
   and you both don't really dig flying
   and it's hard to take off from work
   with bills to pay and things to do
   and it's even harder
   to put things in the past

Well life on the Sun is a lot different
   than living on a cool planet like Earth
   people here don't go outdoors much
   so, it's very much a technological society
   you can be sliding down the holographic solar flares
   one second
   and diving deep into the virtual magma pools
   the next

They say that the Sun
   keeps getting closer to Earth
   so, I guess we'll be practically neighbors soon
   I'm not exactly sure how you feel about that
   but it wouldn't kill you guys to have an open mind
   about interspecies relations, time-travel, spaceships
   and forgiving one another

one day, it'd be nice to get everyone back together
wishful thinking, I know
but nowadays anything's possible

I have to go now, but I really hope
    you both make the trip sometime soon
    and as always

Take Care
    With Love,
    Sincerely Me

# Untethered

When I disconnect, I will fly untethered
Inside veins, where my ancestors still flow
They were romantic and hopeless
Inevitably, I jumped two times
Finding no peace, just open space
As I take flight again, I pace my soul
To ease my uneasiness about what I desire most
And yet if I were the ellipsis in your sentence
Causing you to pause…to consider
Never fitting in and always being a certain way
Stepped out of your world, fully brave
Metaphysically awake and conscious of oneself
In the future, talking to ghosts in the present
Conditionally they wait for us
To expire from these temporary constraints

And if, I could take two steady breaths in succession
And not think of my sorrow
I would raise the corrupted condition of my people
Become Baldwin, MLK, X, or Medgar Evers
A raven's laugh is heard distantly
You might say I am under siege and a lost cause
Suffering from a terminal system failure
But my friend, be wary of tomorrow
For, I will likely storm the Middle East
Cause the Sahara to sink in its sand
Capture Agape love in a thought
Just to send it out
with the cool, cool wind

## Wisdom in the Low Sunset

Once I gained all the knowledge I needed
  I found my youth was gone
The road I left behind
  had become impassable
    or had it always been this way?
Was I the Beast
  leaping from this overgrown path?
With only base instincts
  and no thought of tomorrow
It would explain
  how I disregarded the thorns
    and survived the jungle floor
When I looked into the quieted riverbank
  the fangs I once so proudly bared
    were worn away
How beautifully ironic
  I should acquire Solomon's riches
    only to be contented
      to recline against the sunbaked stone
As the low sunset finds its way
  beneath the impassive, distant horizon

# Three Times Around

**M**uch respect to those who
did it right from the start
but when they said,
"The third time is the charm."
I believe they were talking about me

That First Time
I was not entirely convinced
we both found convenience
she was trying to rebuild
and me?
I was still caught in a past
that had long moved on

The Second Time
was straight rebellion
bandits out to prove everyone wrong
we said I do
in the chapel of our living room
baggage and insecurities
were the gifts we exchanged
the escapade of us was displayed
like an inner-city mural
on an abandoned building
our inevitable demise
was met with indifference

The Third Time
    was unexpected deliverance
    I had finally come to terms
    with the balance of things
    and by chance
    rediscovered a soul that took me back
    to a time before the colors faded to gray
Like water from the sky
    we easily fell into place
    late night conversations
    about different choices, what ifs,
    and how many kids we might have had
    only to realize through our reflective paths
    that we were perfected for one another
At last, there is no need to redo life
    not if there is a chance of missing this moment
    not when there is a chance of missing being
    loved completely

Much respect to those who
    got it right the first time around
    but when they say,
    "The third time is the charm."
    know that they are talking about me

## Already Written

Read the chapters of my life
  from right to left
Start at the tenth chapter
  and you might feel
    subtle envy

By the fifth chapter
  the protagonist's role has shifted
    and you may feel somewhat unsettled
Do not be troubled
  I will tell you now
    the next chapter
      was already written

It took every bit of perseverance
  for me to complete this fourth chapter
And even though
  I am almost at the halfway point
    my youthful impatience
      still finds its way into every line

I continue on
  the foreshadowing contained
    in those middling paragraphs
      promise an unexpected pivot
So, I see myself through
  the center leaves
    unable to turn back
      I am bound to this path

I will confess
   this is not the story
      I would have written
Not the book
   I wanted to read
      I found that you do not always choose
         the words that capture your life

Possibly by the time
   you reach chapter one
      you might see yourself
         in these margins
And find a reason
   to start again
      from the beginning

# The Sport

These distractions were made for Us
Who brought flash to the touchdown,
the handle and finish
A dramatic homerun or a devastating combination?
Running faster than
What was thought to be possible
To have purpose in the Sport

Within the crowds
What did we seek?
Love, acceptance, power, or wealth
In return, we are expected to remain silent
And accept the curses thrown our way
We are both warriors and concubines

If not for the Sport,
Who would be our Master?
What Nation might we make proud?
Reality is cruel
And adulation is seductive and blinding
So, while we are still champions
For another generation
Let us hail and bask in
The Sport of Us

## An Idealistic Dream

Remembering my previous life
  is like recalling the sounds
    of a fading dream
On most days
  I fill in the gaps
    with reasoned thoughts
On other days
  I'm the child
    Who'll continually find a way
      to animate the objects
        laying about the room
When you're of this mindset
  you'll always find a way to save others
    but never find time
      to save yourself
Nevertheless, I still hope it's possible
  that my unconscious dreams
    survived the crucible of time
And find a way
  to self-assuredly walk
    without strings attached
      back into this idealistic life

# Gone

You were here, but now you are gone
You were here, your last words undeniable
You were here, before I told you everything
You were here, but now you are gone

Here you are, like you never left
Here you are, now explain what you meant
Here you are, and so quick I am lost again
Here you are, like you never left

I was here, but now I am gone
I was here, my last words undeniable
I was here, but you never told me everything
I was here, but now I am gone

# Walking Away

Excuse me if I do not participate today
In the destruction of the world
It is fallen and slowly breaking apart
Tomorrow, I may leave
Until then
I know you may call my name
And if you do
I will likely become part of this dark tapestry
But today
The respite of that future tragedy
Temporarily soothes like chamomile
Enjoyed in the presence of a quiet wind

I close my eyes
And choose not to see America's true face
I cover my ears
So not to hear the sirens as they close in
I continue to walk away
As they shout out
To join in
To lay down
To unmask
To distance
To be a mindless consumer of today's cause
To be another
Faceless victim of tomorrow's unrespited law

# Finding Forgiveness

**H**ow are you, my friend?
Back then
The roads we chose ran on parallel tracks
Despite this insurmountable distance
I hoped our destined paths would intersect again

As for me
The vines of empathy
Made it difficult to cut the ties
And the walls I built ultimately failed
To stop the involuntary reflections
Ironic how estrangement and time
Soften even the hardest memories

My friend
I do not know much about your life
As it is now
Too much time has passed
For me to claim that kind of knowledge
Still, I imagine you kept moving away
Never stopping to look back
When you eventually arrive
And meet your destination
I wonder if in that place
Will you also find
Your forgiveness?

# The Space Between

Whenever, she turned away
The moon sent his light
They were in space
It was not much he knew
A reprieve from the scrutiny of the day
Filtered light
Cool and nonjudgmental
He needed to believe
That even when her sky was full
She still desired him
In her, there was life
And the reason for his existence
Touched by the heavens
She held substance and air
They were in space
He could never get close
Fated to watch from afar
Such is the life of a solitaire
Beautiful is the curse of a star

# Imperfection

Your voice is beautiful
Its imperfections divine
Let it falter
Let it blow
Speak out loud
Be wholly confident
In what you say
No one else
Sounds like you

## Nearly Fell Apart

I was an inaudible decibel
  of my former self
    after almost falling apart
Created a deft persona
  to ward off the psychosis
    and to survive the impending trials
Unnatural how one season
  stole the summer's warmth
And if there was such a thing
  as an alternate reality
    I might step through that veil
      to see how it might have been
In this life
  I tried to turn back time
    with prayer and fasting
That fastidiousness eroded
  into curses and drink
On Today, I understand
  how an idealistic mindset
    caused me to wander away
On Today, I fell
  into a deep slumber
    and dreamed the kind of dream
      only a dreamer would chase
On Today, I thought to call
  to say something
    after all, I nearly fell apart
      thinking of you

# Sound of Truth

Your voice
Covers me like waves
Gently kissing August sands
Lost at sea
Persuasively carried away
By the tone of your truth
There is more beneath
Here the undercurrents
Are without pretense
Surrounded in bliss
Completely captured
By the sound of you

## Inside the Machine

The pain is not totally apparent
  Understandable
Since most days you are not completely alive
  So, you do not notice
  The gears pinching and pulling
  Specifically programmed
To fit your every groove
  To push your life forward
Even on your worst days
  You are forced into place
  Choose not to synchronize
  And
  Be
  Systematically
  Broken
  Down
From a distance
  Those disconnected parts
  Are indistinguishable from the scorched material
  Hard to see ourselves down there
  On another day
  I would do more
On another day
  I would stop to help
But today
  I am unable to process
  Empathy
  Inside the machine

# Accepted Orbit

I am only fragments
Pulled together by the unseen
Colliding with your atmosphere
And the pieces
Start to pull away
As I fall into space
It should be known
That I was not made for this world
Here, the air has kept too much in place
Escaped those snares
And gathered the remaining pieces of my spirit

Today again
I collided with the truth of this world
And again
The fragments of my life
Burned brightly across the dark sky
Holy is the name of the gravity that kept me
And yet and still
In fact
More than anything
I wanted an accepted orbit
Most of all
Above everything
I desired
To be like you

# The Edge

It is on the edge of your lips
A dangerous situation waiting to be taken
Today, I anticipate the words
Might just build
Tenuously hang
And finally fall
But again
You perfectly balance the conversation
A vexingly precise tightrope act
Imagine one day that you might slip
And softly descend into my safety net

Today, I apologize for my future absence
When I leave this circus
For another show in town
How you fell on that day
Hear it was the most beautiful mistake
Ever made
Sobering that I will never exactly know

Fully matured through the high and lows
I want to believe there was joy in that moment
But was there disappointment?
That I was not present on the day
The loveliest words, ever spoken
Finally fell

# A Letter of Thanks

To my Ancestors
Thank you for surviving the traumas
The physical and mental horrors visited upon your life
I am your legacy and if you chose not to continue
I would only be a notion whispered by the winds
Something that would have been
Lost forever
If not for you

# To see the Truth in October

It was a clear October night
We had been looking up for some time now
I wanted her to get lost with me
And absently said, *Can't you see.*
To which she presently replied, *No.*
Turned away
Before, the moisture coalescing in her eyes emerged
Maybe, I was asking too much of her
After all, the nearest star was approximately
4243 light years away
Yet she was much closer
In the chill of autumn
My arm felt the warmth
Hopelessly far-sighted
Focused on what was furthest from me
Found her to be mostly obscured
Against the backdrop of a limitless universe
The truth of our positions
Revealed on a clear October night
And we both silently said to ourselves,
*There will never be another night like this*
*… you should really try and see*

24

# Love Got Me

Love got me out here
I mean really out here, ya'll
Ready to do whatever
Like my life don't matter at all
Ran into a burning building
Hoping to save everyone
Knowing how those type of scars, tend to stay
Wanted to stop the recycling of today's tragedies
And if I could somehow save love
Then maybe life for you would also change
But my good intentions were wasted

Standing across this gated lot
Where the littered memories of our past
Still float about
Know that it's love
That got me fucked up
But also know, I would've suffered more
To shield you from the truths of this life
I wanted to say
That love's inexplicable, unmistakable
And also heartless
It's not a safety net
There's no guarantee of reciprocity
In fact, there's no surety at all
And those sanguine scars will remain
Long after the shadow of love
Fades away

## The Source

The blood that lives in me
Gives my ancestors a chance at salvation
Most had the strength to persevere
But some were troubled souls
And a few even knew bliss here on earth
So, I try to balance their post-traumatic notions
With the wisdom they acquired through life and death
I might be unqualified to act unilaterally
But they can only be passing thoughts
So, I suppress their instinctive urges
And the generational curses embedded
In those thoughtless tendencies
They know not what they do
I am saving their lives
By perfecting mine
In time, I too will call out to my successors
And demand to be heard and counted
After all
I am the source
And through them
Life will be perfected

## Plastic Forks, Knives, & Spoons

**B**ack then
It was simple to see her
Behind the glass pane
She lived in a different world
Still every day
I walked to work and imagined
If I could buy some of her time
Take her out to lunch
Gain her understanding on where she stayed
On issues like Creation
Cafés in France and Plastic Forks, Knives, and Spoons

Wanted to know her in a different way
However, I could never step foot in that world
As time slipped away
I could only stand and watch
As a properly attired caller confidently asked,
*To be shown only the best.*
One by one, they were beautifully presented
He remained unimpressed
Until his eyes fell upon
What was to be mine
And yet, I wondered
If he would take her out on first dates
Or care to gain her understanding
On where she stayed
On issues like Creation
Cafés in France and Plastic Forks, Knives, and Spoons

As life would have it
One day, I found her waiting
She was no longer surrounded by luxury
Her edges were not quite as smooth
Still, her pull was no different than the moon
Speaking so only she could hear
I told her of my travels
And my endless search for extravagance
From the most exotic places
And after all this time
I needed to know her
To gain an understanding
On where she stayed
On issues like Creation
Cafés in France and Plastic Forks, Knives, and Spoons

## To Write It All Down

**M**y rough draft was far from refined
Recklessly spilled letters onto the surface
Words appearing after some time
But what could they say?
In silence
They will lay
Unless they are put together
Cohesively
In silence
They will stay
Until they connect to a life
Coherently
Arrange a phrase
To express a thought
A sentence
Slowly emerges
Forming the edges of a philosophy
That articulates a belief
Chapters build
Becoming fully developed now
A manuscript to endure on
Even as the author fades with time
There will be a peaceful victory
Within these pages

# Legacy of Slavery

I can describe with words almost anything
Still
I am unable to fully capture
The essence of my African and American self
I fail to adequately express
So, I compartment the unspoken words
That would illustrate those daily offenses
But in doing so
I further incarcerate
My most innocent and creative thoughts
And this oppression is the greatest crime
Of this whitewashed legacy
I deflect praise
I cannot be great

# Judgement

Yesterday
Judgement came to visit
And I wondered
How long would it stay?
I smiled hoping for the best
Perhaps at one time
You might have looked at my life unconditionally
However, lately it has been only lukewarm embraces
And canned conversation
Pains me to say the least
I want to offer you a thought
And in turn listen to your new ideas
But the past insults create an intense air between us
And the unspoken words blur your face
You are barely there
I pause and see someone new
Regrouping my senses
My eyes keener now
After all these years
You finally become clear

# Water Takes Shape

She can be all these things
Like water you take shape
So easily
What river pours from within?
*Impatience*
Never waiting to know if it is a sin
Caught in this overflow
A Slave beneath this heat
Diligently sowing
Unseen seeds
In hope of a harvest that will erase my tattooed mistakes
And drown my mortal regrets in the deep
Easily you became all things
My Answer
Effortlessly
Water takes shape

# Fifty-Nine Seconds

It is the end of the world
…and there are only 59 seconds left
To breathe, to love, and to curse the day

What if there was no reason
To lie, cheat, or to make a fool of love?
As the ground falls apart
So easily
You find that hate was a choice
Yet so was love
When there are only 40 seconds left
To breathe, to love, and to curse the day

Ordinary moments now become so much more
When the moon breaks orbit
And the oceans are no longer contained
There are ten seconds left
Do you still care
To hurt
To complain
To see the difference
Or do you just want more time?
The end of all we know and now…
There is only one second that remains
To breathe,
To love,
And to curse the day

## The Park

We will not be here for long
So, enjoy yourself
Look out for friends and strangers
They are always close
Consider the idiosyncrasies that pull at your beliefs
See the waves crash with your own eyes
Listen carefully, but seek the truth alone
Travel like the wind
Knowing you are never far from home
Let the magic momentarily suspend you
And remember the illusion when it fades
Know this place could never stay the same
So, enjoy yourself
We will not
Be here for long

# Counterfeit

It would be wrong to say
That a counterfeit comes first
There are no hard rules in life
Know a falsity can come late
These things cannot answer the simplest of questions
As transparent as the waterways of the Missouri River
Their origins are difficult to ascertain
Twisted like an image held too long

To be sure, the truest will never withhold a word
As you explore the depths of their sea
You will find no boundaries
Solve the most difficult questions
And conquer so much more

Counterfeit, tell me.
What value is there?
When nothing, I can know
Fills that space
It would be foolish
Like trading air for gold
When air is life
While gold is a heavy burden
That loses its shine

## The Hunt

**I**'m not afraid
Just don't wanna be on anyone's mantle
It's the Year of the Gun
And from the looks of it
You don't need a permit to kill
So, as they stalk
I'm keenly aware of their intent
For us there can be no missteps
When every shot penetrates
They never seem to miss

As the media broadcasts
The stirring images sinking us to new depths
The despair of our ancestors is remembered
We protest and trust—it's live!
But there's no amount of justice
That can return a soul to life
In that moment of tribulation
I'm sure
      All anyone
                         Wants
   To do
            Is to

Keep
     Breathing
Simple and God-given
Yet and still
They hunt

# Seventeen

Remembering how
We had so much energy to dance
On rhythms that never grew tired
Warm sweat got in-between
Like birth, the world was wide
It is that way
When you have only lived that far

To have been with you at seventeen
Would have been illmatic and new
Ironic, this album cover with its worn edges
Caused me to ask
What could have been?
If not for the pull of my friends
And the cool vibe of the strip at that beach
If those things
Were not everything to me

Holding you close was fresh
Listening to Kane and Stetsasonic was dope
You knew all the dances
All the while, laughing at me
Always with bad timing
Like a New Jack Swing
Energy surrounded us
Somehow, we missed pictures
No Polaroid to remember us

We lived outside any 4 x 6
No regrets on that
However, your prom picture with my replacement
Has given me
The keenest sense of melancholy
Know it is hypocrisy
To say that life was unfair
Know it was my decision
To miss remembering you at seventeen

# Dear Georgia

The first time in size eleven boots and fatigues
I ran away
And the last time I left
You hardly noticed
I get it
We were both war weary
No tarnished medals, citations
Or worn ribbons of the great shit I did
Could possibly compensate for our PTSD
After all, we were just trying to survive

Georgia, you were always humid
And always on my mind
Thick
Deep
And heavy like the air
Thinking about all the times
You carried on
Like a song sung at the banks of the Savannah
We were Spanish moss swinging in the twilight
Even so
It is easy to become detached
It is easy to fall

Being robbed of every treasure
As I was
An old hat
Me telling that story when I was whole
Always thinking of my three
Funny, how I lived without indemnity

39

Now trapped by time and the frames that led to this life
The reel does not pause or rewind
There are no roads that lead back to Georgia
And if I somehow got lost
Fate would find a reason
For me to leave again

# Who, but You?

**W**ho made the choice?
To conquer and subjugate an entire continent
For capitalistic gain, making millions landless?
Who enslaved the red, brown and black?
Categorizing a race of people as sub-human
Who were the men that sailed across the Atlantic?
In search of new lands to claim
Was it you?
Who terrorized and lynched?
Soulless eyes destroying homes
Degenerating countless for hate's sake

The evil that ensnares men is inherited
And also learned
Pray earnestly, my friend
But know, forgiveness is only given to the repentant
And while some sins are harder to escape
Some are easier to hide

So here we are
Subjects to the curse that resides in man
And if evolution is still a proven falsehood
Then we can only wait
For the knee of the oppressor
To be precisely positioned and pressed
Against our exposed necks
As the minutes, then seconds
Of our lives
Expire

# A little bit less

That rose was not for you
Yet
It sits alone
In your tinted vase
Cool water at its base
It is already dead
Today
I cannot hide my face
Want to confess that I am not in love
I know you will not read the signs
I also know
You cannot keep it alive
Because everyday
It is a little bit less

# The Comedian

**W**hat is behind that laugh, funny man?
You eased your way around the audience
Evading the reality of it all
The happiness you gave freely
Somehow escaped you
Unforeseen behind that mask…gloom
Today, the jester has turned its back on the crowd
Out of character, you silenced the laughter
Tonight, there will be no more improvisations
Farewell, spaceman
We cannot follow you
Yet I wonder
Did you smile or attempt one last laugh?
Before you drifted off into that endless night

*~ In memory of Robin Williams*

## Soul Advocate

At times
It feels as if the compartmentalized traumas
Have been passed on to me
And in turn
I spend most of my day
Repressing those voices
While trying not to relive
Yesterday's ordeals
My ancestors want justice and to be free
So, when it comes to writing
I do not believe
I ever had a choice

# Soap and Opera

Understanding before I knew
Learned how life could be played
Every mid-day, they came alive
Was there really this world
So unlike my own
Yes, because here they were
Restless and young, beautiful and bold
So many dark shadows
They would crash, burn, then rise
Heartbroken and still alive
No one was truly dead
Inanimate things
And me, who felt compassion for the rock and the leaf
Became captured by the interplay
Wondering what it meant
Felt it was worth imitating
For a time, they loved, fiercely
Yet, their love was never faithful
Confused, I was still a child
Promised to never be like them
But in time, I grew into the script
Written to fill an hour
Not much more
My life fully developed
Now imitating the art of drama
Brought to you by your favorite commercial sponsor

# Finis

**A** simple thing, I ask
The cast are all in place
And the performance will begin soon
What I will ask, after all this time
Should not be a hard thing to do
From behind the curtains, the audience is restless
You stand there, anxious
Although, we have performed many times before
Your eyes seem dilated
Adorned with intricately placed flecks of sienna
Your lips slightly part
Brushed expertly with a deep shade of carmine
In character, I say evenly
*After our last kiss,*
*When the curtains close,*
*You will walk away and not look back.*
Predictably, tonight is standing room only
They have all come to witness our final act

## Unapologetically

**I** started then restarted again
I loved then found love again
You hated and reasoned to hate again
   Do you remember the look you gave?
   When I found a steady pace
   You could only see behind me
   And I — was only beginning
   To see life as it is
   Like a wave set high above the shore
   I wanted you to understand
   The burden I carried

With time, I became like the cirrus
   Aloof and indifferent
   Here above it all I found
   Most of the answers
   And they were neither right nor wrong
   Instead like the Mississippi
   They are like us
   Inexplicably muddied

After soaking in the idiosyncrasies
   I was able to escape freely
   into the atmosphere
   Like water rising from the sea
   I am unapologetic
   And without regret
   As I consider
   What I left behind

# The River

What river runs from your soul?
Is it wide throughout?
Or does it narrow in certain places?
Tell me will there be dry seasons
In the most southern waters
The storm approached
And the waves became insurmountable
Avoiding the conflict
I set a course for the northwest
After a month away, I became lost again
Strong currents overpowering this vessel once more
Felt the rapids when the surface became troubled
Ignored the signs
High off these greenish blue reflections of you
As I neared the boundaries
My captivation becomes insanity
The rush, the deafening sounds
As the waters fell
I was tempted to look ahead
Before forcing my eyes away
I found the courage to accept the inevitable
After all
A lifetime can be had
Within the fall

# Ikigai
## (Translated: That Which Gives Your Life Purpose)

This happens on certain days
At my desk a new favorite playlist, shuffled
My attention is dedicated, focused
Intending to work,
When a moment of insignificance
Triggers a thought that opens a door
There is an *imoye,* which provides clarity
A new gravity that pulls me away
A message to deliver, a portrait to paint
How do you capture the unseen?
When words are no more than a dirty lens
A lost archaeologist
Carving thoughts into stone
Fingernails are torn
They are numb
The pain left long ago
After five hours of scratching the surface
I am beginning to understand

It is 1:31 in the afternoon
The new playlist has worn on
The reports are partially done
Fortunately
I am not the only one
In this office
Searching for Ikigai

# Humidity

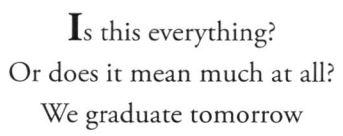

Is this everything?
Or does it mean much at all?
We graduate tomorrow
Then there is college in the fall

At this moment
I cannot imagine that life
I just want to ask
That you stay with me
On this fifty-yard line
After the band leaves
And the game is lost
There is no need for us to rush away

Soon, we will have a lifetime of regret
Before we are called
I want to ask you so much
But this humid small-town air
Stifles everything

# A Cursed Species

**R**acism is the reason
Why I do not believe
Humans can ever evolve

It is clear
That this kind of hate
Is native to only one species

## The Aquarian

This empathy has led to dysfunction
Words that were not my own
Escaping from my lips like smoke from a fire
No surprise
That the ancestor of a runaway
Ran
Natively, sunk to the level of my roots
Planted tightly into the cracks
Of this broken and uneven concrete
I felt the soles of every traveler
Weary from being enslaved by their dreams
Desired to be the smoke floating above the pyre
Instead, I feel the fire
And see the true nature of man
To be set apart is necessary
Isolated from the empathy
That has secretly replaced
So much of me

## Sketching You

It is still not perfect
These hands have not been steady for awhile
Takes longer to trace the lines
There have been so many erasures
And now the paper wears thin
Consequence of holding on to every mistake
I will turn the page eventually
But for now
I am slowly finding a way to capture her smile

# Eden Paradox

The life in my veins knows its true nature
And try as I might
The things I should do
Do not come easily
Like Man reaching out to control
What was not given
Forbidden
As are the fruits of flight, the moon and stars
Artificial life, and the knowledge of war
Like paradise walking away
I was responsible
Yet
I prayed Eve chose to stay

# Comprehension

And the Light shineth in Darkness
The Darkness comprehended it not

After a time, he remained in the dark
Still, she was unable to recognize him

The Light stopped the fear
From creeping into his life
Yet, she did not know this

He found that the Light
Helped him endure the loss
Despite this
She waited for him to fade

So, when he left
She, the Darkness
Comprehended it not

# To Get Back

**I** was born to be a Soldier
If you asked, when did I know?
I would say it was the day
When I didn't have enough to buy food
And I looked into my little girls' eyes
That's when I knew
That I would be on that next plane
Fighting someone else's war
In a foreign land
Now, back on familiar soil
Here alone
I'm fighting the demons that I left behind
But you should also know
That I'm living
To get back home
To my little girls' eyes

# Highway to Heaven

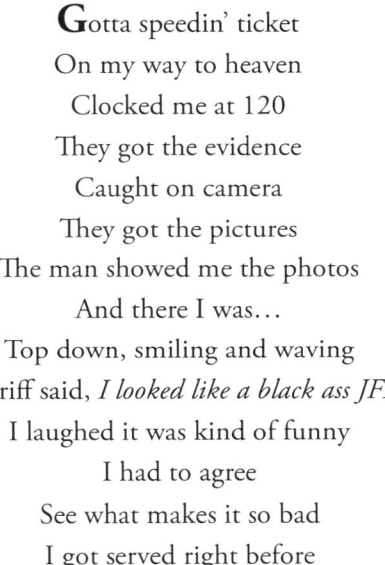

Gotta speedin' ticket
On my way to heaven
Clocked me at 120
They got the evidence
Caught on camera
They got the pictures
The man showed me the photos
And there I was…
Top down, smiling and waving
Sheriff said, *I looked like a black ass JFK*
I laughed it was kind of funny
I had to agree
See what makes it so bad
I got served right before
I could put my black ass
Inside those pearly white gates
Handcuffed and arrested,
No Miranda Rights today
Should've seen the look on my face
Drug me downtown
Gave me no time to change

So, there I stood
In all white
The Judge
Yea Him
In all black
Entered my plea of Not Guilty

But Mr. Honorable was not tryin' to hear none of that
Pointed at me and then turned to the bailiff
And said,
*That today, oh today*
*I'm gon learn that in the Commonwealth*
*All Negroes eventually will burn*
So, with a grin
He gave me another lifetime
Eyes to the sky
I said, *Lord, you know I don't deserve this*
Kept out of heaven for a vehicular sin
So, if you happen to be on that *Highway to Heaven*
And you see me in all white picking up the trash
Don't let my current situation get you off track
Rejoice, laugh, wave…shit even put the top down
But whatever you do
Don't
Drive
Fast

# A Game for Two

Sit down love,
There is a game to be played
Only two of us here
To put it simply this evening
The rules will not be explained
You looked surprised
But now, you exude Las Vegas cool

Easy to tell
You have been here before
By the way the cards easily slip through your fingers
Was it the smart shuffle, the divide
Or how the cards snapped to attention?
All of which, just further heightened the anticipation

I cut, you deal
And of course, we start fast
After a while
I get wide-open
Carelessly show my hand
Forgetting you were heartless
Should have known my King of Hearts
Would never stand a chance

For the first time tonight
The fullness of your deep red lips
Can be entirely appreciated
The pair slightly curl in at the corners
You have been waiting for a while now
And this felt like certain victory

I nod in recognition
A pretentious flick of your wrist
And in slid the Queen of Diamonds
The last of the royalty
I stared for a moment…what was it?
Possibly, I was captivated by the crown
Or saddened that this game was at its close?

One last card to be played
The lowly Deuce of Spades
However, tonight this pawn was wild
And at the slow recognition of this fact
You begin to object
Then, you remembered our first rule
Which we both knew all too well
In a game of love
Someone must win
And someone
My Queen…must lose

# Pillar of Salt

**A**s I prepared to leave
You show me your best
Although the sky above you
Is dark and full of sulfur

# waiting for your notes

**W**rite me
a song
quiet and pure
tell me with notes
about your pain
your dreams

write me
so, I can orchestrate
all of the pieces
the horns, strings, and percussions
in flawless synchronicity

only care to play
your song
so, write me soon

# Breathe Easy

**B**reathe easy
Let go of your struggles
Don't think
Life's too heavy
Lay your cares down
Breathe easy
Don't think
Just lose time
Lose tomorrow
Live only for today
Breathe easy
Don't think
It's too much
Hold onto today
Quiet your mind
Breathe easy

*Thank you for reading*
*Sparrow in the Machine*